PROJECT:  STEAM

MUSIC
THE SOUND OF SCIENCE

DR. MARGARET E. ALBERTSON & PAULA EMICK

Rourke
Educational Media
rourkeeducationalmedia.com

Before Reading:

Building Academic Vocabulary and Background Knowledge

Before reading a book, it is important to tap into what your child or students already know about the topic. This will help them develop their vocabulary, increase their reading comprehension, and make connections across the curriculum.

1. *Look at the cover of the book. What will this book be about?*
2. *What do you already know about the topic?*
3. *Let's study the Table of Contents. What will you learn about in the book's chapters?*
4. *What would you like to learn about this topic? Do you think you might learn about it from this book? Why or why not?*
5. *Use a reading journal to write about your knowledge of this topic. Record what you already know about the topic and what you hope to learn about the topic.*
6. *Read the book.*
7. *In your reading journal, record what you learned about the topic and your response to the book.*
8. *After reading the book complete the activities below.*

Content Area Vocabulary
Read the list. What do these words mean?

amplify
diameter
frequency
mallet
physics
reflected
sound waves
vibrates
vocal cords
wave period

After Reading:

Comprehension and Extension Activity

After reading the book, work on the following questions with your child or students in order to check their level of reading comprehension and content mastery.

1. *How do vocal cords work?* (Summarize)
2. *How might music be different without scientific knowledge?* (Infer)
3. *What types of technology are used to create music?* (Asking Questions)
4. *In what ways can music affect your mood?* (Text to Self Connection)
5. *How do string instruments produce sound?* (Asking Questions)

Extension Activity

Find a place free from distraction. Listen to different types of music and write down the way each song makes you feel. Think about why the music evokes these feelings. Is it the tune, the lyrics, or a combination? Next, think about why some scientists would want to study the effects of music on human emotions and behavior. How could that knowledge be used to help people?

TABLE OF CONTENTS

STEAM MUSIC

Turn on the radio. Crank up a song. Can you hear the science? How about the math?

Musicians rely on the STEAM subjects—science, technology, engineering, art, and math—to make music.

Some scientists study **sound waves**. Technology is used to make computer-generated sounds, and improve instruments such as electric guitars. Engineers use scientific principles to design new instruments, amplifiers, and sound equipment.

Artists write music and lyrics to tell a story or share emotion. Mathematics is used for counting beats and to compose harmonies and rhythms.

Let's Experiment

Gather:

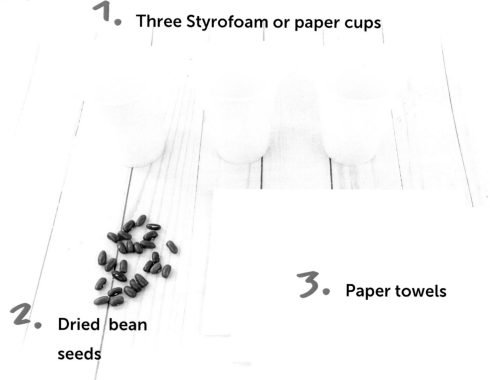

1. Three Styrofoam or paper cups

2. Dried bean seeds

3. Paper towels

Do:

1. Put a dried bean seed in each of the three cups.

2. Put a folded wet paper towel on top of the beans.

3. Place the cups in three different places, away from each other. Wet each towel daily.

4. For one, play music three hours each day. For another, play music for one hour. For the third, play no music.

Observe:

Track the growth of each sprout over two weeks. Is there any difference? You can also experiment with different types of music.

SOUND WAVES

The snare drum, in front, makes a short, crisp sound.

How do you hear a drum beat? Tap a drum. The top **vibrates**, or moves back and forth. Vibrations push the air, forming sound waves, which travel to your ear. You hear the drum beat.

The science called **physics** is the study of matter and energy, including sound waves.

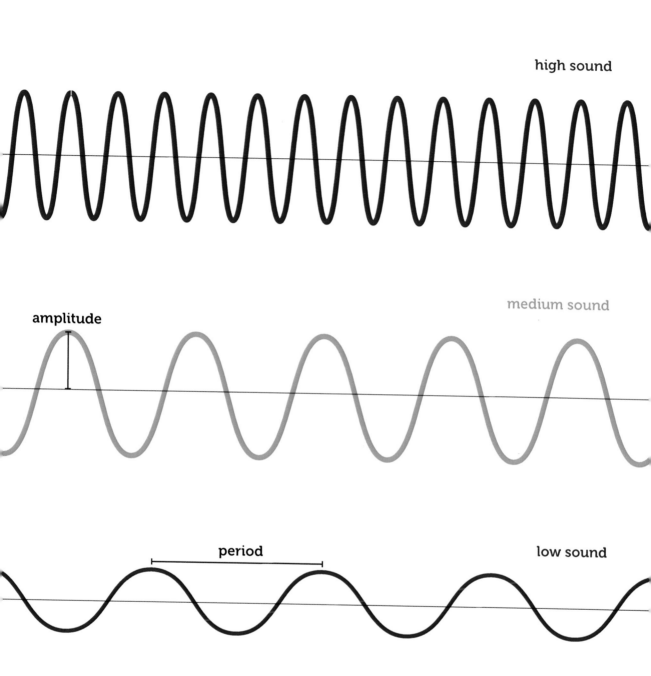

high sound

amplitude

medium sound

period

low sound

Musical notes are made of sine waves. The diagram shows a wave's amplitude, or strength. Loud sounds have greater amplitudes than quiet tones.

The picture also illustrates the **wave period**, which is the time for one vibration. Higher notes have shorter periods than lower sounds.

An oscilloscope measures sound waves. Making sounds into a microphone turns the sound waves into electrical waves. The oscilloscope projects these onto its screen. There are apps that use a computer as an oscilloscope.

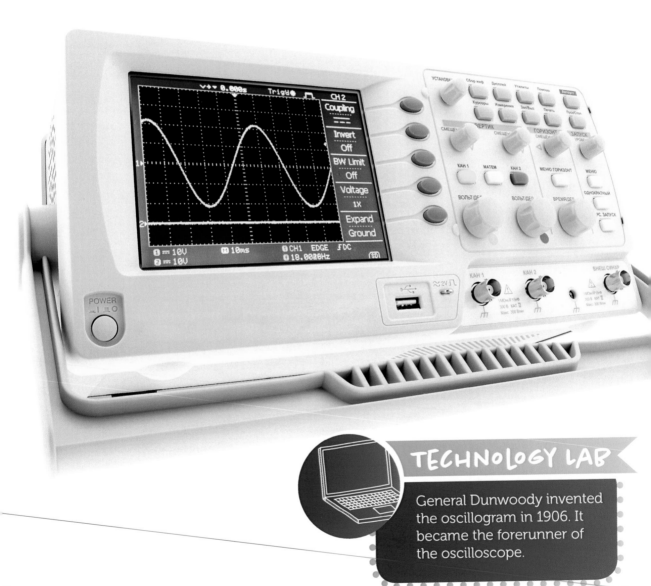

TECHNOLOGY LAB

General Dunwoody invented the oscillogram in 1906. It became the forerunner of the oscilloscope.

See a Sound

Virtual Oscilloscope

This online virtual oscilloscope allows you to visualise live sound input and get to grips with how to adjust this useful. our online spectrum analyser may also be of interest to you.

Physics   Sound   Audio

An oscilloscope is a useful tool for anyone working with electrical signals because it provides a visual representation of the signal's shape, or waveform. This allows it to measure properties of the wave, such as amplitude or frequency.

The initial signal above is a 200Hz sine wave, which has an amplitude of 5 volts. The frequency of this wave can be adjusted by using the "Input Wave Frequency" slider. (You can also choose to display a square wave.)

If you are browsing using the latest version of Google Chrome, the input dropdown box allows you to select "live input". This will take data from any microphone

Gather:

1. Computer or tablet with microphone

2. Another computer, tablet, or cell phone

3. Internet access

Do:

1. Go to any website with a free virtual oscilloscope application. One option: www.academo.org/demos/virtual-oscilloscope.

2. Download a signal generator to your second device, or use an online version such as http://onlinetonegenerator.com/.

3. Play the signal generator loud to quiet and low to high.

4. Freeze the sound wave on the oscilloscope before you change the signal.

Observe:

How did the sine wave change when the tone was loud? Quiet? Low? High?

As you made the signal louder, it became stronger, pushing more air. On the screen, the waves had more amplitude, so they were taller. Louder sounds have greater amplitude than quieter sounds. When you changed the signal higher or lower, the wave's speed changed. High tones vibrate faster than lower tones and have shorter wave periods.

VIBRATING STRINGS

Artists can feel the musical vibrations as they play the guitar.

Guitars and violins make sound with vibrating strings that push the air forward, forming sound waves. Different musical notes are made by changing the string's thickness, length, and tightness.

A 440

An orchestra tunes to A 440 (pronounced "A four forty"). The oboe sounds this tone, and the other instruments match it.

How fast the string vibrates is the **frequency**. The musical note "A" equals a frequency of 440 vibrations per second.

MUSICAL NOTES

There are seven musical notes: A B, C, D, E, F, and G. Each has its own frequency. C 4, the scientific notation for "middle C," is about 261.7 vibrations per second.

Rubber Band Guitar

Gather:

1. Cardboard shoebox, lid attached

2. Empty 16.9 oz. (500 ml) water bottle

4. Glue

3. 7-inch (17.78 centimeter) rubber band

Build:

1. Glue the bottle about two inches (five centimeters) from the short edge of the box.

2. Stretch the rubber band longways around the box and over the bottle.

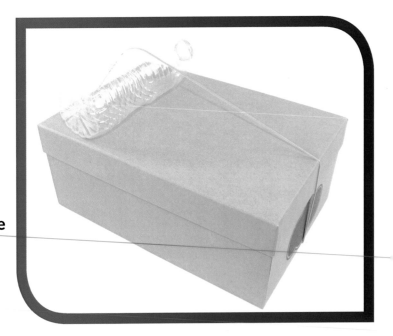

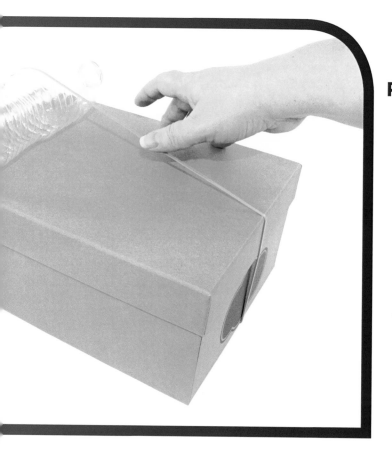

Play:

1. Pluck the rubber band's long end.

2. Slide your finger up the rubber band pressing down against the box lid. Pluck the band.

3. Pluck the rubber band's short end.

Observe:

Compare the rubber band's sound between the long and short parts. How did the sound change?

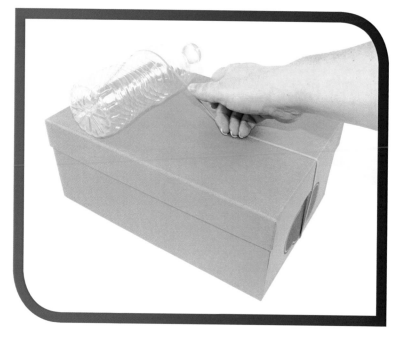

When you slid your finger closer to the water bottle, the notes became higher. The rubber band was tighter and shorter, so it vibrated faster. Likewise, the shorter part of the rubber band near the water bottle sounded high because it is shorter and tighter.

Voice Acrobatics

Gather:

1. A virtual oscilloscope like the one used in See a Sound (page 9)

Do:

Sing a familiar song in different manners:

1. A very high voice.
2. A very low voice.
3. Loud and quiet.
4. Squeaky or silly voices.

Observe:

Freeze the screen while you are still singing.

How do the waves compare?

You have **vocal cords** in your throat made of folds of membranes. The vocal cords vibrate when air passes through them.

tongue

vocal cords

trachea

Vocal cords are part of the respiratory tract.

Vocal cords change sounds when they vibrate at different frequencies.

Squeaky and high singing tighten the vocal cords, making them vibrate faster. The faster traveling waves are closer together. Normal to low sounds vibrate slower. Their waves are further apart.

The volume levels show differences in amplitude. Louder sounds spike higher than quiet tones because they have higher amplitude.

BELLS AND CHIMES

Although bells and chimes are usually made from the same materials—metal, glass, or pottery—they're shaped and played differently. Bells are larger at the bottom, smaller at the top, and are usually struck from within. Chimes are tubes or rods and are hit from the outside.

SCIENCE LAB

Chimes, xylophones, gongs, glockenspiels, cymbals, hand bells, sleigh bells, and cowbells are musical instruments.

Glass Xylophone

Gather:

1. Three glass drinking glasses

2. One spoon

Do:

Fill each drinking glass with water:

1. Three-fourths full **2.** One half full **3.** One-fourth full

Play and Observe:
Tap each glass with the spoon. Which glass sounded highest? Lowest? Medium?

DO

RE

Challenge:
Try to make the glasses sound like "Do, Re, Mi" by adding and subtracting water. Tap the high (Mi), then the medium note (Re), and then the low note (Do). That is the beginning of the song "Mary had a Little Lamb." Try playing the rest of the song.

DO, RE, MI

Singing "Do, re, mi, fa, sol, la, ti, do" is a musical exercise called *solfege*. Invented by Guido de Arezzo in the eleventh century, it is still used to train musicians.

Why did the glass with the most water sound low?

When you hit the glass, it vibrates. These vibrations travel through the water and into the air. This makes sound waves. The more water, the lower the sound. Subtracting water makes the tone go higher.

Charming Chimes

Gather:

1. Metal teaspoon, tablespoon, and serving spoon (chimes)

2. Wooden spoon (**mallet**)

3. Coat hanger

4. Tape

5. String

Build:

1. Tape string to the handle of each spoon.

2. Tie the other end to the coat hanger so each spoon hangs down.

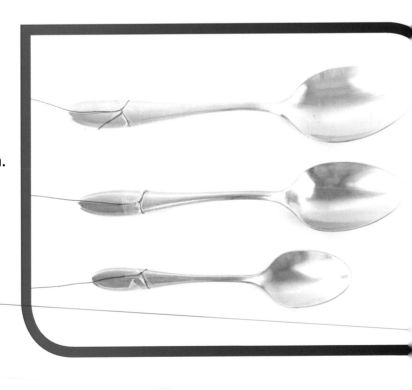

Play:

1. Hold the coat hanger by the hook.

2. Strike the spoons.

SCIENCE LAB

When struck by a mallet, the chime vibrates. A longer spoon sounds lower because it vibrates slower. The shorter the chime, the higher it sounds.

Observe:

Which spoon produces the lowest note? Highest? Middle?

TUBES

Flutes are made from tubes. Blowing over the top of the tube vibrates the air, creating an air column.

Flutes can be made from metal, glass, or wood.

MUSIC STUDIO

You can turn tubes into musical instruments. You need a tube with a small opening. Blow across—not into—the hole. With practice you'll play a tone.

Panpipes have been played for thousands of years.

Panpipes

Gather:

1. Three drinking straws that can be cut

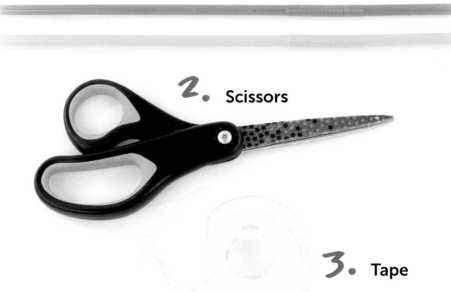

2. Scissors

3. Tape

Build:

1. Cut straws about three inches (7.6 centimeters), five inches (12.7 centimeters), and seven inches (17.8 centimeters) long.

2. Lay the straws sideways in a row from shortest to longest. Make sure they're even at the top.

3. Tape together.

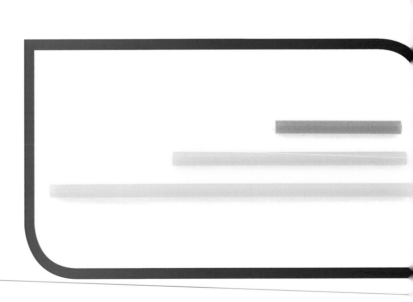

Play:

1. Blow across the even end of each straw.

2. Place your finger over the bottom of each straw while blowing.

Observe:

Which straw was lowest? Highest?

How did the sound change when you covered the bottom of the straws?

Blowing over the straw vibrated the air column inside, producing sound waves. The longest straw made the lowest note because the sound waves had to travel a longer distance. Higher sounds came from the shorter straws because their air columns were shorter.

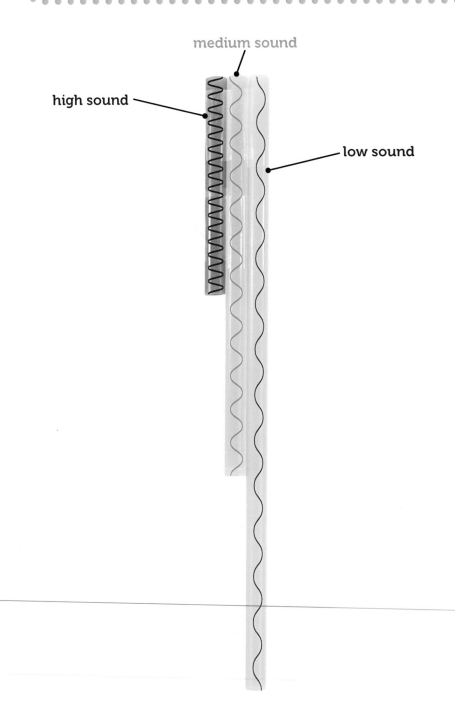

medium sound

high sound

low sound

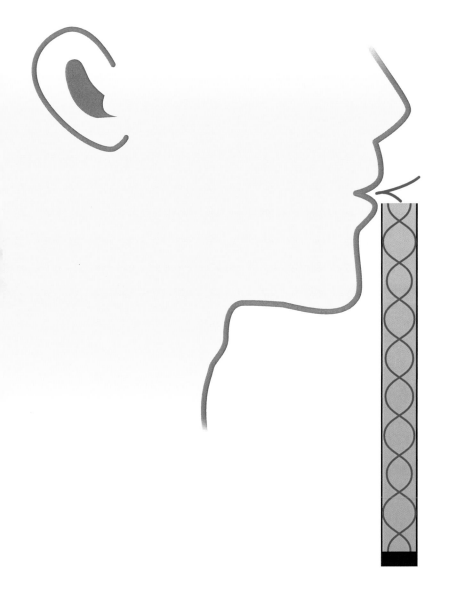

When you placed your finger over the straw, the air vibrated downward, touching the closed end, then **reflected** back the same distance up the straw. The sound waves in this closed air column traveled twice as far as when it was open—no finger over the bottom. Because the wave traveled longer in the closed column, it sounded lower.

Bottle Band

Gather:

1. Two-liter soda bottle
2. One-liter soda bottle
3. 20-ounce (591 milli-liter) soda bottle

Play:

1. Hold a bottle straight up and down.
2. Blow across the opening.
3. Move the bottle up and down until it makes a tone.
4. Repeat with the other bottles.

Observe:

Which bottle sounded the lowest? Highest?

Wind from your lips blew across the bottle's opening, vibrating the air column inside. Sound waves traveled the farthest in the two-liter bottle, so it sounded the lowest. The 20-ounce bottle sounded highest because it had the shortest air column.

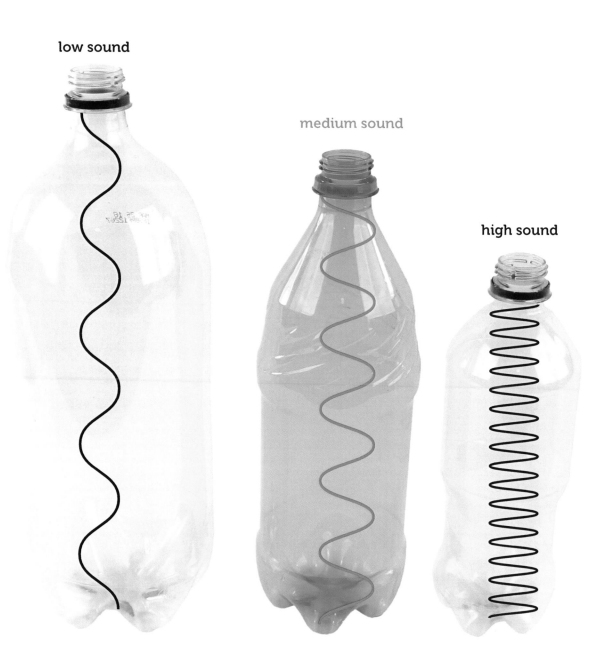

low sound

medium sound

high sound

BUZZING

Musicians blow into brass instruments through buzzing lips.

Buzzing Horn

Gather:

1. 20-ounce (591 milliliter) soda bottle

2. Paper towel tube

3. Marker

4. Sharp heavy-duty scissors

5. Tape

Build:

Mouthpiece:

1. Insert the neck of the bottle into the tube.

2. Trace around the tube with the marker onto the bottle.

3. Cut neatly along the marked line on the bottle with an adult's help.

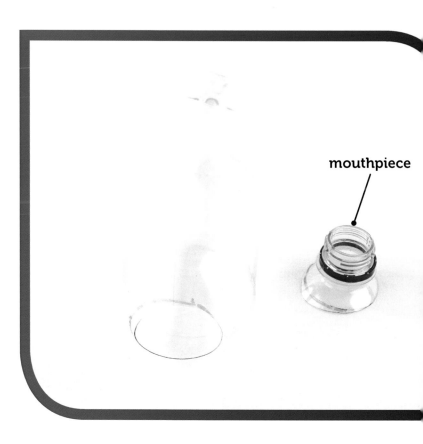

mouthpiece

Bell:

1. Draw a line around the bottle, about three inches (7.62 centimeters) from the cut edge.

2. Cut along the line carefully with an adult's help.

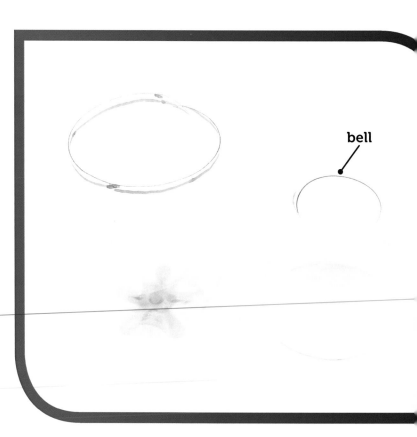

bell

Assemble:

1. Tape the mouthpiece onto the tube's opening.

2. Tape the bell's small end to the tube's other end.

Play:

1. Blow into the mouthpiece while buzzing your lips.

2. Change your buzzing by using loose, tight, and tighter lips.

bell

Observe:
How did the sound change when you buzzed your lips differently?

mouthpiece

33

The tone that comes out of trumpets is louder than the buzzing sound that went in, because their bells increase, or **amplify** the volume.

Your buzzing lips send vibrating air through the mouthpiece. This sets the air column in motion, creating sound waves that exit from the bell.

When you buzzed your lips loosely, the air column vibrated slower, creating a lower sound. The tighter the lips, the higher the tone.

A trumpet might seem short and compact, but when unwound it stretches to about 5 feet (1.52 meters)!

PERCUSSION

Musicians play percussion instruments by tapping, striking, or beating. They use their hands, sticks, or mallets.

The piano is a percussion instrument because each key pulls back a mallet, which strikes a metal wire.

A piano has 88 keys. Pianos made before the early 1970s had keys made of ivory. That's why some people still call playing a piano, "tickling the ivories."

Beating Drums

Gather:

1. Different size clean, dry, empty cans, 16 ounces (500 milliliters) or larger

2. Two wooden spoons

3. Scissors

4. Can opener

5. Packing tape

Build:

1. Remove the bottom of each can with a can opener.

2. Criss-cross tape over one open end of the can.

3. Continue until the whole opening is covered with two layers of tape.

4. Turn the drum over and press down on the tape.

5. Secure ends by wrapping tape around the can.

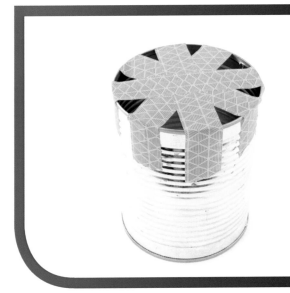

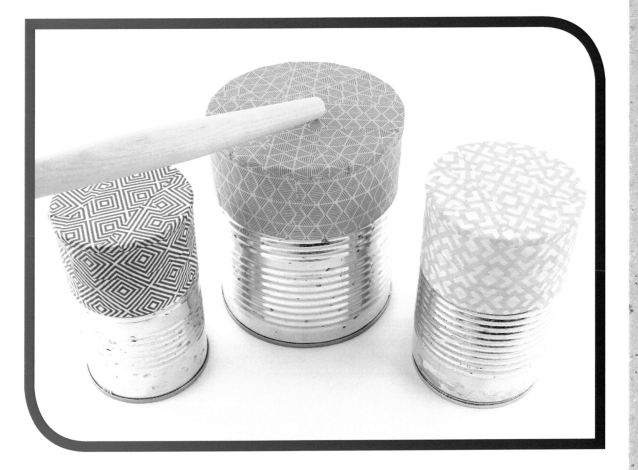

Play and Observe:

Use your hands and wooden spoons to play your drums. How does the sound change with the drum's **diameter**?

A drum called a timpani can be tuned to specific notes. The drum's top skin is stretched or loosened to change tones. The tighter the skin, the higher the sound.

The drumhead vibrates when hit. This sets the air column inside the drum in motion, making sound waves with a high amplitude or loudness.

Increasing the diameter of the drum makes the sound waves longer. The larger the drumhead, the lower the sound.

A timpani is also known as a kettledrum.

Rain Sticks

Gather:

1. Construction paper

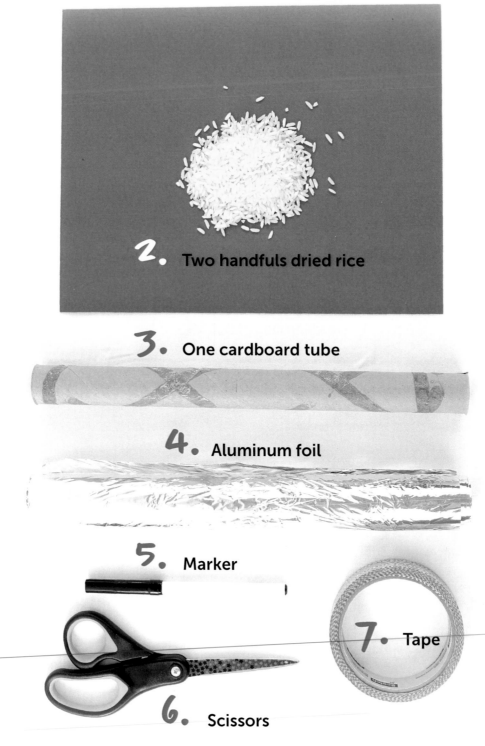

2. Two handfuls dried rice

3. One cardboard tube

4. Aluminum foil

5. Marker

6. Scissors

7. Tape

Build:

1. Twist foil into spirals.

2. Fill the tube with them.

3. Trace tube end twice to make two circles.

4. Tape a circle to seal one end.

5. Pour rice into the tube.

6. Close the tube with the second circle.

Observe: Watch and Notice

Lift the tube straight up and down. Tilt the tube down until the rice starts to move. Listen to the rain sound.

As rice falls down the tube, it strikes the foil many times. Each time it hits the foil, it makes a tapping noise. With lots of rice falling, the tapping becomes almost continuous, making the sound of rain.

Rain sticks are percussion instruments because the sound comes from striking. Some cultures in dry climates made rain sticks from dried cactus tubes, hammering needles into the inside and filling them with pebbles. They used these instruments in ceremonies to call for rain.

LET'S PLAY MUSICAL CHARADES!

First, make a drum with the instructions on page 38. Then gather some friends and form two teams. One team thinks of a song and taps it on their drum. The opposing team gets three chances to guess the song and win a point. Then it's their turn to tap out a song. The team with the most points wins.

45

GLOSSARY

amplify (AM-pli-fye): to make a sound louder

diameter (dye-AM-uh-tuhr): a straight line passing from side to side through the center of a figure, especially a circle or sphere

frequency (FREE-kwuhn-see): the number of vibrations per second in a sound wave

mallet (MAL-it): a hammer with a rounded head used to play a percussion instrument

physics (FIZ-iks): the science that studies matter and energy, including sound waves

reflected (ri-FLEKT-ed): sound returned from a surface

sound waves (sound wayvz): vibrations in air, water, or a solid that can be heard

vibrates (VYE-brates): to move back and forth repeatedly

vocal cords (VOH-kuhl kordz): bands or folds of membranes in the larynx, which vibrate and make sound waves when air from the lungs passes through them

wave period (wayv PEER-ee-uhd): the time for one cycle of a sound wave

INDEX

SHOW WHAT YOU KNOW

1. Explain how sound travels.
2. Discuss how wavelengths and sound are related.
3. In what way does the size of an instrument affect its sound?
4. How can you change an instrument's sound from low to high?
5. How are percussion instruments different than air column instruments?

FURTHER READING

Johnson, Robin, *The Science of Sound Waves*, Crabtree Publishing, 2017.

Royston, Angela, *All About Sound*, Heinemann, 2016.

White, H., White, D., *Physics and Music: The Science of Musical Sound*, Dover Books, 2014.

ABOUT THE AUTHORS

Margaret E. Albertson, Ph.D., a music specialist and pipe organist, and Paula Emick, an art specialist, enjoy teaching and writing for children. In their spare time, they enjoy traveling and spending time with their families. They both reside in Southern California with their husbands.

www.rourkeeducationalmedia.com

PHOTO CREDITS: Cover & Pages 5, 12, 13, 17, 18, 19, 20, 21, 24, 25, 26, 27, 28, 29, 31, 32, 33, 38, 42, 43, 44: © creativelytara; Page 4: © Merlas; Page 6: © Fatihhoca; Page 7: © Andrii Shelenkov; Page 8: © Llepod; Page 9: © AlexAndrews; Page 10: © g-stockstudio; Page 11: © cyano66; Page 14: © DragonImages; Page 15: © solar 22; Page 16: © Wylius, © rimglow, © kaycco; Page 22: © lisegagne; Page 23: © IvoneeW, Neyya; Page 30: © 3drenderings; Page 34: © monkeybusinessimages; Page 36: © Furtseff; Page 37: © creativesunday 2016, © DFTidrington; Page 40: © Olaf Speier; Page 41: © Trodler; Page 45: © Wanda_Lism; Additional Illustrations: © digimann, © ilyast, © AllAGRI

Edited by: Keli Sipperley
Cover and Interior design by: Tara Raymo www.creativelytara.com

Library of Congress PCN Data

Music: The Sound of Science / Dr. Margaret E. Albertson & Paula Emick
(Project: STEAM)
ISBN 978-1-64156-463-2 (hard cover)(alk. paper)
ISBN 978-1-64156-589-9 (soft cover)
ISBN 978-1-64156-705-3 (e-Book)
Library of Congress Control Number: 2018930489

Printed in the United States of America, North Manchester, Indiana